Life Between The Breaths

short series of poems on mental health

NICKY

BookLeaf Publishing

India | USA | UK

Made with ❤ on the BookLeaf Publishing Platform

www.bookleafpub.in

www.bookleafpub.com

Dedication

To my dog Simba and my mother who adopted her for me.

Preface

We all have similar yet different lives yet we search for ourselves in the tiniest things. We stumble across poetry for the same reason: that someone somewhere is experiencing what we are experiencing, that someone somewhere will say or make us believe that we are not alone.

When I suffered from my very first panic attack, my family and I thought that I might get a heart attack, asthma, or corona therefore I ended up in the emergency department of a pulmonologist. Don't worry it is not a medical book. Consequently; I'll not get into what happens during anxiety in the body and brain biologically or biochemically. There is plenty of information available online and to your doctors.

It is also not a help book for the patients. This book is more for people who are suffering from anxiety and think why me? Who thinks, am I the only one?

This book is especially for people who are not suffering from anxiety. It is required that they get to know what an anxious person might go through. I am not claiming that every person has the same experience as we all are the same yet different in this physical world. But even reading about one experience, one can help their loved ones and the suffering person will find solace.

Believe it or not, whatever society claims mental health is still taboo and society doesn't take it seriously. Moreover, some people use the term 'anxiety' so casually while not knowing what it feels like. Exam stress = anxiety panic attacks; practical viva = panic attack; fight with boyfriend = anxiety, scolded by parents = anxiety panic attack, bad day = anxiety, panic attack.

NO that's not how this works. Anxiety kisses you softly at times when you just spent the best day of your life and now you can hear your heart pounding so hard that you are losing breath. And now anything negative or even slightly violent seen, heard, or thought of will trigger it to a near-death experience while knowing you will not die from this but you feel like you are definitely going to die.

"Hamare time m asa kuch nhi hota tha" ("in our time these things didn't exist"), "ye tumhari generation ki problems h, hmare paas to time he nhi tha asi cheeze sochne ka" (these are the problems of your generation, we didn't have time to think about such things"), "arre don't think too much just chill have fun you will be fine", "doctors want to make you their permanent customer, therefore, exercise every day this will go".

There are plenty of such dialogues but I'm not blaming anyone. I think your loved ones want to help you but they just don't know how. Because there is a lack of education on mental health just like there is a lack of

education on some of the most important aspects of life such as menstruation, Sex, etc. Doctors also help to a certain extent. But how long will you have to be dependent on medication?
This book is also for me. I'm writing this short series of poetry, to let my heart out, my mind out, to give one more feeling, one more experience in this ocean of experiences,

for you, for me, and love.

-Nicky J

Acknowledgements

It is my great pleasure to present this *short series of poems on mental health* to my generous readers. It is gently influenced by my experiences of suffering from a mental health disorder known as *'anxiety neurosis with panic attack disorder'* which according to psychiatrists is like 'flu' in their area of study.

Flu takes time to go away but it goes away, while anxiety is uncertain like life. I hope this book will meet your expectations and you feel even if no one at least I am with you.

I would like to extend my deepest gratitude to the ones who have been a part of this journey with me.

Starting with my *father* who took me to the doctor. A typical Indian hard-working dad. But he understood what happened. He made me feel like it was the most important aspect to deal with. He did everything he could with an open mind.

To my *mother,* who slept in my room for days to make me feel safe. Who till now rubs my back, and chest whenever I get a panic attack.

To my *brother,* who always makes me laugh in the most unlaughable situations to soothe me.

To my *dog Simba,* who unknowingly has been a blessing in disguise. Her mere presence is enough to make me feel better. She seems to understand everything. I find her a wise lady.

To my *Snow White* for taking care of me when no one else does. For being one constant in this uncertain life.

To my *psychiatrist* who has walked this difficult journey with me and shown me the light to which I can reach.

I extend my special thanks to my mentor *Mr Sushil Manav*, a remarkable journalist with over 35 years of experience working with leading publishing houses. He has not only enhanced my writing skills but also gave me wings to pursue my interests. At such a mature age, such an energetic individual can make anyone motivated. I am blessed to meet a person like him in this lifetime.

To my mind and heart for finally initiating the compilation of this piece, lying in some corner for years. Finally, my greatest gratitude to you. May you find that hope, solace, tranquillity, that light of which we are in search of.

1 . AN ANXIOUS MIND

Sitting all alone
I am feeling so sleepy
All dead and deaf
I must go... go in deep sleep
Till its ending
But where is the ending?
Is it going to end?
Or is it just the beginning?

2. AN ANXIOUS SEARCH

2

Wanna run toward that last beam of light,
Which is soon disappearing right in front of my sight,
It is becoming more and more dark here,
For I don't care or no one else cares here.

3. THE SEARCH CONTINUOUS

Light, light, where is thy Light?
Or darkness is the reality,
Light is just sight?

4. PARADOX

Days turn into nights,
One after the other,
What if in every world I go,
Darkness is the only thing we share in common!
Ideas, strength, knowledge, and love, wait for me in the darkness.
Whilst light only brews competition, judgment, fear, and hatred,
Will I ever be out of this paradox?
Or this paradox is reality and everything else is just a myth.

5. AN ANXIOUS REALITY

They say everything is destined,
Everything is planned here but still unplanned,
Everything Is certain here but still uncertain,
So, what to believe in and what not?
What is real and what is not?

6. THE ONE

Everybody consider themselves the best ,
The know it all,
Whilst I consider myself as a nobody,
A continuous learner perhaps,
Even if all is one,
That one seems very lonely.

7. A DEPRESSED MIND

And then they say
How can you be depressed here?
For you have everything
What more could you want here?
What shall I say to those dispassionate souls?
For I have no words to express my breathless soul,
When my heart beats a thousand times faster without
any drug or alcohol,
And I just keep waiting for my next breath beside these
shores.

8. A DEPRESSED THOUGHT

For some, I exist,
For some, I don't,
Nothing really matters if I exist,
Nothing really matters if I don't.

9. SOMETIMES

Sometimes I look in the mirror and say who am I?
Sometimes I don't recognize myself,
Sometimes I feel what am I doing here,
Here in this body,
Sometimes I wonder why anything is happening,
Sometimes I get scared of myself
Like I am some stranger, to me?
Sometimes all at once.

10. DIARY ENTRY - 11/07/21

It is a deep, dark space. I don't know if the light is even real or just a mere illusion like almost everything. We are fed from our childhood about that light in various names, which we are searching for, but where is it? Or what is it?

In a world where every organism is fighting for life, where every species is in a race for its perfect evolution, I find it very difficult.

Maybe that's why we are scared of death. Even if you try to crush an ant it runs for its life, but what is it getting by living? Is it just because of her sheer love for life? Or is it to find some kind of perfectness like us?

If somebody crushed me like an ant today, I would not run away, I'd die happily it's just that I don't dare to do it by myself nor do I have the courage to live it. I'm hanging in between and it is terrifying here.

I have everything, I'm not poor or in any kind of financial crisis. We are a nuclear family. My parents and my little brother love me to death. I even have a dog named "Simba J, my mother brought her for me when I was diagnosed with anxiety.

I don't know about the condition of my anxiety right now because that's the beauty of this disease, you never know just like life but 'it will not kill you' as per my doctor's words. I think it's not gonna kill you but it's only gonna make you suffer more.

Even without any disease the thoughts that come across my mind remain probably similar. The truth is, that I find absolutely no meaning in anything neither in the luxuries of this world nor in its devastation. I think of myself as nothing and the same for everybody else. It is a simple thought process either you are nothing or you are everything or even if there is something in between that seems very far to reach.

Is living the only way to reach it? I try every day to have a purpose in my life but eventually, every purpose doesn't make any sense anymore as we are going to die therefore, we will never know if the purpose was the thing called life.

So now what? Should I make a pseudo purpose, live my whole life working for it and when I die I'll know absolutely nothing?

I am at a certain stage where I don't find happiness in anything. I don't even want to be happy because I know nothing in this world can make me happy and I know nothing is permanent but still I want to be in between happiness and sadness.

The truth is that we will never know still we become part
of this fancy illusion like fools not living at all.

Sometimes I think, am I thinking too much sometimes I
curse myself for being in this situation, and sometimes I
wonder why I have this mind that is thinking constantly
about something not known by most of us and why it
just can't live happily doing work like others and die in
peace eventually. But at the same time how, what I'm
thinking is too much as this is the basis if I do not think
I'll be an absolute ignorant of everything.

People on the spiritual path call it good to look inside
and have these questions but it is very tough, as more I
get to know or understand things the more I find that I
know absolutely nothing and everything is senseless.

11. FEAR

I stand at one reality,
Life slipping through my fingers,
Has it happened before?
Yet I stand each day in front of the mirror.

Same me, physically aging,
Biologically aging,
Surroundings are changing,
New friendships love in making,
Yet I'm still here in front of my mirror.

So many people dancing,
Gulping this nectar or poison of living,
I know the future, I will still be standing,
Like this unknown, from the truth of reality,
Is this a cycle? Or is this just one life?
"Why" is my ask.

Not known scientifically or philosophically,
So many life forms have lived and died,
Lived and died again and again and again,
Yet I stand in front of my mirror.

Same me same you,

Don't know where we're heading,
You call it fear I call it a quest,
I can live and die happily,
But for what?

12. SLUMBER

In slumber I find peace,
Deep in my mind,
Where logic loses,
I look for answers recklessly,
Thus, do not wake me up
O lover!
Let me sleep, let me sleep, let me sleep.

13. AN ANXIOUS OBSERVATION

"Tranquillity seems transient."

14. CHESS

A rendezvous of thoughts,
What one should do..what not ....
I have the strings of my brain lying down entangled,
know not how to disentangle them.
Should leave them in distress or
Should I start playing the game of chess...

15. CONSISTENCY

"A good brain Is a live example of great practice."

16. AN ANXIOUS CONCLUSION

I am feeling all alone again,
Again and again, I end up like this,
Compelled to look back a little bit,
I thought I had made enough friends,
But at this moment solitude is with me
Not any friend!
Wouldn't it be nice if I made solitude my friend?
Loving him, adoring him with no complaints and
restrains!
Before
Naïve me feared you
But now
Wise me knows
The truth, the bliss is you!

17. search for love

Even if you are alone, not lonely,
Even if you are far from the chaos of the world,
Even if you like your own company,
Even if you understand the gist of the working of this
universe,
Still your soul crosses miles in search of love,
As if you yourself are love
And love is your home!.....

18. AN ANXIOUS LOVE

How much you love me, he asked
I chose life over death for you,
That's how much I love you. She answered.

19. SELFISH LOVE!

22

I never knew how selfish I was until I met you.

20. LOVE

When I saw your eyes,
For the very first time,
They frightened me,
As they were a lover's sight,
'Me' my brain wondered!
For it had never known such a gaze,
That can't be found in a thousand lives,
Yet you were standing there,
Like a magical knight,
And I....I ran away,
From that morning bright,
But you never give up on me,
With your intentions right,
How can someone be more myself than I am?
I finally understood Brontë's lines,
I don't want you to be worried,
Of my fearful mind,
But when my heart beats high,
And my brain creates an anxious sight,
You still stand beside me with your charming smile,
Will I ever be enough with this frightened mind?
For you have indebted me for this lifetime.

21. THE WAY

Love is the only way in,
Love is the only way out.